D0391631

Dear Friend,

LETTERS FOR YOUR
SPIRITUAL JOURNEY

Dear Friend,

LETTERS FOR YOUR
SPIRTUAL JOURNEY

By Sandy Beach

Edited by: Patricia Charles
Design: Karin Badger

ISBN: 978-0-9909020-0-3

Printed in the United States of America
First edition

Published by
HOTCHKISS PUBLISHING
17 Frank Street
Branford, CT 06405
info@HotchkissPublishing.com

*T*hese writings are dedicated to those who came before us: the generations of brave souls who sought the spiritual path in spite of the distractions and pressures of the world around them. Because of their courage, dedication, inspiration, suffering and joy of sharing, we now are surely closer to the light. God bless them all.

Dear Reader,

I have prepared these letters to you in the hope that you will use them
to partake of spiritual nourishment on a weekly basis. We all have
busy schedules, and the demands of family, work, friends, and other
commitments swallow up our free time. Perhaps you don't think you
can afford the luxury of spending time on your spiritual side. The
truth is, you can't afford not to do it. Most of us never realize that
a steady starvation of our souls is at the heart of all our difficulties.
Instead, we conclude, time after time, that our problem stems from a
lack of money, respect, a good relationship, sex or a new car.

This book will help you conduct a very practical and simple
experiment on yourself. Each week, you will read and contemplate a
new spiritual message. On the following page, you will find a sample
worksheet that will give you some ideas about how to go about chart-
ing your own weekly plan. I hope that you will direct your energies
toward this most vital area of your life. The rewards are great. And
you deserve them!

Very frankly, it is essential that you observe closely the personal
transformation that will start taking place in your life as you follow
these simple steps. As you begin to balance your spiritual needs with
the other pressing matters in your life, changes will occur. Ultimately,
it will be your awareness of these changes, and of an accompanying
spiritual power flowing in your life that will give you the faith to continue. As you consistently give nourishment to the essence of yourself,
your spiritual nature, all other areas of your life will miraculously be
made better.

—Sandy

A sample Weekly Journal entry for a message on letting go and letting God.

My Initial Thoughts To This Week's Message:

"I believe this will help me. I need to do this. I am under a lot of pressure. I commit to starting each day with 10 minutes of prayer and meditation, asking God to take my burdens. I will try to stay focused on letting go all throughout the day. Try to cheer up others at work. End day with another 10 minutes of prayer."

Daily Reflections:

Monday – "7:30 A.M., sat quietly, prayed, and read weekly message 3 times. Imagined my day in a letting go mood. Day went well. Quiet time again at night."

Tuesday – "7:30 A.M., read message and meditated on its purpose for me. Calm all morning. Lost it briefly after lunch. Five-minute quiet time in office and felt better. Quiet time at night."

Wednesday – "Late for work, no time for quiet time. Morning was a hassle. Remembered to take book to work and read message over the lunch hour. Went to Fred's office and tried to cheer him up over his wife's illness. Quiet time at night."

Thursday – "Reading and quiet time morning and night. I must continue this. I am sure it is working."

Friday – "Late again, forgot book. Too many meetings. Bad day."

Saturday – "Sat quietly in backyard for 30 minutes. Read message and thought about its meaning for me. Good day. Prayed about letting go at night."

Sunday – "Quiet time morning and night. Boy, it's hard to overcome selfishness. I resolve to keep trying."

Week's Conclusions:

"I know I made some progress. It seems as if part of me does not want this to succeed. I should buy a book on meditation. I pray that I will continue. I look forward to the next message."

Dear Friend,

LETTERS AND JOURNAL PAGES

Weekly Journal: Freedom

Initial Thoughts:

_____

_____

_____

_____

_____

Daily Reflections:

_____

_____

_____

_____

_____

_____

_____

_____

_____

_____

_____

_____

Week's Conclusions:

_____

_____

_____

_____

Dear Friend,

As you read this, you are doing something that does not come naturally, nor easily to us – namely, trying to move from the physical realm to the spiritual. While it may be true that you just "happened upon" the path in the first place, you are to be heartily commended for your dogged persistence in continuing the journey. Your example will inspire many others to follow. You are part of the current flowering of spirituality in this world. Many thirst for what you are seeking.

Along the way, I'm sure you have encountered the contradictory qualities of a spiritually-guided life. Let's look at one of those qualities today: freedom. Many of us think it would be nice to be free to do "anything we want." But would it? Would we be truly happy if we were free to live just as we pleased? What would you choose to do? Go skiing every day? After a few months of this, you might wish you were at the beach. Six months at the beach, and you begin to want something else. Eventually, you might begin to suspect that meeting your wants does not guarantee happiness.

I am sure you have guessed it, Dear Friend. True freedom is achieved through spiritual discipline. Freedom is not the accumulation of options, it is the elimination of them. It is not about meeting the demands of our wants; it is the elimination of the wants themselves. Spiritual discipline brings us closer to our Creator and, thereby, closer to the awareness that everything is precisely as it should be. We are then free to be totally in the now.

Weekly Journal: Self-Worth

Initial Thoughts:

_____

_____

_____

_____

_____

Daily Reflections:

_____

_____

_____

_____

_____

_____

_____

_____

_____

_____

_____

_____

_____

Week's Conclusions:

_____

_____

_____

_____

_____

Dear Friend,

How nice it is to have a friend like you, a person with a heart of gold and a desire for a better world. You try so very, very hard, and I'm sure it seems that others rarely recognize your efforts. Please know that your daily struggle does not go unnoticed. Every step you take along the way is appreciated. You are loved beyond your dreams. There is so much to you, so very much. You matter and you count. Success cannot occur without you. You are a key player in the overall plan for the world. You have so much to contribute, and all of us are better because of you.

Be good to yourself today. Let your heart sing. You deserve no criticism; you are doing the best you can right now. Look around you and see the world that God has prepared for you. See the sky and the seas and the mountains. See the trees and the birds and the wonders of our modern age. Relax in the realization that you are not in charge. You are here by design, and you are exactly where you are supposed to be. Hear the sounds of your world. Listen to the music, the waves, the voices, the thunder, the whistling of the air and the sound of your own breath. Smell the fragrances of your world. Enjoy the aromas of baking bread, Italian food, French perfume, salt air, bacon frying, roses in bloom, and the soap you use.

Dear Friend, the world is grateful for your contribution to it. You are a child of God, and you are surrounded by God's grace. We cherish your smile, and we acknowledge your divinity. You are important, and your talents are unique and God given. Thank you for being you.

Weekly Journal: Perspective

Initial Thoughts:

_____

_____

_____

_____

_____

Daily Reflections:

_____

_____

_____

_____

_____

_____

_____

_____

_____

_____

_____

Week's Conclusions:

_____

_____

_____

_____

Dear Friend,

For those among you who are just beginning your spiritual journeys, it might be worthwhile to look at some basics that have been passed on by others who have trekked this road in earlier days. I hope you find them useful.

First, we must understand that the purpose of a spiritual journey is to change our personal reality. In other words, the actions we take will cause us to see everything differently. Our world may still be the same, but we will see it in a new way, one we may have only dreamed of before.

Next, this change will be accomplished not by learning anything new, but rather by unlearning or relinquishing the old. The truth about ourselves already lies within us. We were born with it. Our task here consists of fearlessly taking stock of our old ideas. Then, we must spiritually discard them while at the same time fully embracing the fact that reducing the ego will always be a painful process. Remarkably, out of this arduous process itself comes the joyful awareness that a loving God truly exists within us.

Finally, we eventually see the purpose of spending time in prayer and meditation each day. This time deepens and widens a channel to our inner spirit that lovingly flows outward toward others. This is a simple task, but it must be pursued each day.

Overcoming the self is the greatest challenge in the world. Know that you are worth it. The Spirit of the Universe waits with open arms to embrace you with the reality of your own Divine existence.

Weekly Journal: Awareness

Initial Thoughts:

_____

_____

_____

_____

_____

Daily Reflections:

_____

_____

_____

_____

_____

_____

_____

_____

_____

_____

_____

_____

Week's Conclusions:

_____

_____

_____

_____

_____

Dear Friend,

I'm sure you are familiar with the saying, "You couldn't see the forest, for the trees!" It teaches us that sometimes things are so close and obvious that we miss them.

Many of us become so absorbed in reaching selfish ends that we rarely see the magnificence of our world. Even on the spiritual path, we can experience the "forest and the trees" syndrome. We search for God high and low and wonder why our search has failed. No matter where we look, we come up empty-handed. We begin to wonder if God has a special hiding place, perhaps on a mountaintop in Tibet!

Suppose someone asks you to spend the day observing the prevalence of plastic in your life. As you sit at your desk, you noticed the plastic in your computer and the pen in your hand; at noon, it's the container you brought your lunch in; after work, it's your car, your cell phone, and the credit cards in your wallet; the list goes on. You realize that plastic is everywhere, and yet, you've never really noticed it.

One day, you will get a glimpse of God in a magnificent cloud formation; then, in the beauty of a painting or a piece of classical music that touches you; then, in the power of the waves that crash at your feet at the seashore. Soon, you will come to see that God is everywhere. Once we direct our consciousness to look for God, we discover that everything is God; that God is all there is.

Today, let's look for God in all our comings and goings. If we will only look, we can see God's handiwork in everything and everyone, including ourselves.

Weekly Journal: Surrender Ego

Initial Thoughts:

_____
_____
_____
_____
_____

Daily Reflections:

_____
_____
_____
_____
_____
_____
_____
_____
_____
_____
_____
_____

Week's Conclusions:

_____
_____
_____
_____
_____

Dear Friend,

How nice it is to feel enthusiastic about something! We are suddenly energized and totally focused. At other times, it might seem that we have lost all our enthusiasm for life. Our interest fades, and we feel hurt and lost. We begin to see life as a burdensome struggle, and perhaps the things that used to give us great pleasure no longer have any appeal. Where does our enthusiasm go in these times when it seems to be so lacking?

The dictionary points out that the Greek origin of the word *enthusiasm* roughly translates as "possessed by a god." I'm not proposing that we all become students of ancient Greece, but there is certainly a clue here as to the answer to our dilemma.

Let's look for a moment at how children respond to all of life. From their viewpoint, life is something that automatically inspires great enthusiasm. They are still close to their Inner Spirit and have not yet compromised their vision with ego-centered ideas.

Might our lack of enthusiasm simply be a clouded perspective and nothing more? As we ease God out of our lives in the struggle to achieve ego-driven goals of happiness, we lose the power of our original spirit. Our child-like vision of the world fades into self-centered gloom.

Let's surrender once more to the realm of the Divine Spirit and allow our natural enthusiasm to have its rein.

Weekly Journal: Courage

Initial Thoughts:

_____

_____

_____

_____

_____

Daily Reflections:

_____

_____

_____

_____

_____

_____

_____

_____

_____

_____

_____

Week's Conclusions:

_____

_____

_____

_____

_____

Dear Friend,

Would you describe yourself as a courageous person, or do you think there is something lacking inside of you? Do you often feel that you let yourself down because you lack the "fortitude" to stand up for what is right? Perhaps you believe that your life is never going to change.

Most of us have experienced similar feelings and thoughts at some time or another, but it is important to remember that they are not permanent or true. You have inside you the potential to be your own best friend and to become a hero in your own eyes.

To start with, let's understand that it takes courage every day to continue on the spiritual path. The fact that you are trying to become a better person is proof of a willingness to undergo painful change. Just for today, let's make a priority out of asking God for the courage to take another step away from our past thinking. Just for today, we will refrain from destructive habits and behavior. We will steadfastly patrol our thinking and refuse passage to old and destructive thoughts. At all times, we will stay in contact with our Higher Power, assuring ourselves of protection from our ancient enemy, fear.

We will remain focused on each task at hand and eliminate remorse for the past and fear of the future. With each step that you take along your spiritual way, your confidence will rise. You are no longer alone on your epic journey. You have taken the hand of God, and you are entitled to walk with dignity. At the end of the day's trek, gratefully acknowledge the strength and courage you have discovered within.

Weekly Journal: Honesty

Initial Thoughts:

_____

_____

_____

_____

_____

Daily Reflections:

_____

_____

_____

_____

_____

_____

_____

_____

_____

_____

_____

_____

Week's Conclusions:

_____

_____

_____

_____

_____

Dear Friend,

Did you ever think of honesty as a quest? To be honest with ourselves, we must persevere until we have experienced the truth about ourselves.

When we first start on the spiritual path, our honesty is limited to our current ideas about the world and ourselves. In 1491, before Columbus proved the world was round, people honestly believed that the world was flat. This belief was incorrect. Were they being honest? Of course they were, to the best of their ability at the time.

On our new spiritual path, honesty might be looked at as the willingness to question every aspect of our thinking. It is the decision to forsake our egos and to search for truth at a deeper level. Through the glasses of a self-centered existence, the world may well look flat. But from the view of a God-centered universe, we can clearly see a perfect sphere.

We begin to see that honesty is the acceptance of change. We stop insisting on a controlled environment and place our well-being into the hands of God. In contact with our Higher Power, we become comfortable with the idea that we will always be moving toward truths beyond those we know today. Honesty is the acceptance of the phrase "more will be revealed."

As we approach today, let's wear our ideas loosely so that we may quickly cast them off when deeper truths are revealed to us.

Weekly Journal: Spiritual Progress

Initial Thoughts:

_____

_____

_____

_____

_____

Daily Reflections:

_____

_____

_____

_____

_____

_____

_____

_____

_____

_____

_____

_____

Week's Conclusions:

_____

_____

_____

_____

_____

Dear Friend,

Today, let's think about the spiritual path and what it might mean in our lives.

We all imagine our journeys through life in terms of careers, relationships, fitness, education, travel, hobbies, and many other areas of the material world. But how often do we imagine a journey along a spiritual path and what its goals might be? First, we must realize that progress along the spiritual journey results in a transformation of the material world itself. As our needs are met through closeness to our Higher Power, our attachment to the material world is loosened.

Clearly, one of the goals of a spiritual life is to set ourselves free from the grip of the world we can see by becoming dependent on a Power we cannot see. We are not abandoning our goals in the material world when we move our efforts to the spiritual arena. We are simply placing them in a new and truer perspective. When our thinking is raised to a higher level, we will intuitively know a superior set of priorities for ourselves.

Our spiritual path does not represent a conflict with our material goals. It offers us freedom from our instinctual demands so that we have real choices. A spiritual path also provides us with a tremendous sense of identity. This occurs as we lose our old ego identity and discover a deeper spiritual sense of being. We discover that our joy of living is a result of drawing nearer to our Higher Power.

Weekly Journal: Ego/Love

Initial Thoughts:

_____

_____

_____

_____

_____

Daily Reflections:

_____

_____

_____

_____

_____

_____

_____

_____

_____

_____

_____

_____

_____

Week's Conclusions:

_____

_____

_____

_____

_____

Dear Friend,

Can you tell your ears to stop hearing or your nose to stop smelling? Can you keep yourself from feeling hunger or fatigue? Can you tell the rain to cease or the waves in the ocean to stop breaking? I think not.

If we can't stop these, then we certainly have no chance whatsoever of stopping our spirits from wanting God. The longing for God is the strongest and most misdiagnosed force in our lives. Because the ego wants no part of a Higher Power; however, it gives us other explanations for our unhappiness.

When our hearts tell us that God is missing in our lives, the ego jumps in and tells us that more money will fix this longing; or more sex; or more power. Its arguments are so persuasive that we pursue each of these goals to disappointing dead ends. Generally, it is only through the process of elimination that we begrudgingly concede that maybe we do need God "a little bit." And thus begins our spiritual journey.

Today, let's allow the longing in our hearts to express itself. Imagine the joy of truly acknowledging how much you want to be close to your Higher Power. Imagine the loving arms of a Universal Mother enfolding you. Imagine being able to experience your true nature.

Weekly Journal: Caring For Yourself

Initial Thoughts:

_____

_____

_____

_____

_____

Daily Reflections:

_____

_____

_____

_____

_____

_____

_____

_____

_____

_____

_____

_____

Week's Conclusions:

_____

_____

_____

_____

Dear Friend,

When we watch a mother with her new baby, we can't help seeing how tenderly she treats the infant. Every movement is done with great care. Her voice is sweet and comforting. She carefully wraps the baby in clothes and blankets that are both soft and warm. She is constantly attentive to the baby's every need; ready to feed, bathe, change, or hold at a moment's notice. Her tenderness serves as a cushion of love between the baby and the harsh world.

Did you ever stop to think how your own life could benefit from the same kind of tenderness? Imagine for a moment caring enough for yourself to provide a cushion of love between you and your world. Imagine your journey through life on a steady smooth course instead of the emotional roller coaster that many of us ride. Is it possible? The answer is yes, of course it is. All that is required is that we learn how to bestow a loving tenderness on ourselves.

Begin today by asking God for the power to treat yourself in a kind and tender manner. When the obstacles of resentment, fear, anger or greed appear in the day's journey, go out of your way to avoid them. Wrap yourself in the warm blanket of your Higher Power and carry yourself gently through the day.

Accomplish the business of the day, but look after yourself with a mother's love. God has charged us with the lifetime care of ourselves. Each of us is the custodian of a magnificent Child of God. Think tenderly of yourself today!

Weekly Journal: Acceptance

Initial Thoughts:

_____

_____

_____

_____

_____

Daily Reflections:

_____

_____

_____

_____

_____

_____

_____

_____

_____

_____

_____

_____

Week's Conclusions:

_____

_____

_____

_____

_____

Dear Friend,

Are you feeling anxious today? You probably would not be human if there wasn't something that your mind had decided to worry about. Anxiety is sometimes referred to as the plague of modern society. In large part, it is caused by the fear that things won't turn out the way we want them to be. Let's look at what we might find along the spiritual path that can help with our anxiety.

First, we have acceptance. Human minds, by nature, have a tendency to control, worry and resent. By simply allowing the mind to run its course, we can greatly reduce its power over us. When a worrisome thought appears, we do not have to dwell on it. We can acknowledge it and leave it alone.

For example, when we exercise, we sweat. That's a fact! Now, if we became frightened because we were sweating and told ourselves that we had to learn how not to sweat, we would never be able to work out again. We can accept sweating and a sometimes worrying mind as parts of life and move on.

Then we can focus our mind on today and our Higher Power. Here, we are practicing the discipline of spirituality. Day after day, we can improve our control over the wanderings of the mind. We can again and again turn our thoughts to God. We can recite prayers and mantras or simply talk with God.

By practicing these spiritual acts over and over, we slowly stifle the power that anxiety has over us, and we open our channel to God.

Weekly Journal: Spiritual Development

Initial Thoughts:

_____

_____

_____

_____

_____

Daily Reflections:

_____

_____

_____

_____

_____

_____

_____

_____

_____

_____

_____

Week's Conclusions:

_____

_____

_____

_____

Dear Friend,

Consider what beauty the flowers of the Earth bring into our lives. Think back on those times when you have stood transfixed by a magnificent field of sunflowers or the delicacy of a single rose.

Let's visualize the process through which a plant grows from a bulb. First, it sends its roots down and pushes its stem up through the soil; it nourishes the leaves and the flower bud. Then, in a singular display, it causes the bud to open. The long-awaited blossom reveals to the world the hidden beauty of God's creations.

So it is with our spiritual development. We prepare the soil within by painfully weeding out the selfish thinking that could choke out the flowering of the good within us. We plant the seed of faith and wait with the confidence of an experienced gardener. We sense the stirring within as the spiritual forces begin to push through our walls of indifference and isolation. We provide daily nourishment through prayer and meditation. We develop patience, which allows the blossoming to occur in God's time.

As the beautiful culmination of our efforts and God's power come to fruition, we are able to open ourselves completely to a loving and personal Higher Power within. We then turn outward and allow our radiance to give witness to others of the undeniable existence of God.

Weekly Journal: Inventory

Initial Thoughts:

_____

_____

_____

_____

_____

Daily Reflections:

_____

_____

_____

_____

_____

_____

_____

_____

_____

_____

_____

_____

Week's Conclusions:

_____

_____

_____

_____

_____

Dear Friend,

Those of us who understand that there is a loving God available to each of us are very fortunate. Amidst the joys and sorrows of our lives, we can always turn to the Great Power within and receive the emotional balance we require to continue on our spiritual course.

In relating to our Higher Power, we might do well to think of ourselves as a water pitcher and of God as the water in the spiritual well. In order to fill our vessels with the waters from the Divine Source, we must first empty the pitcher of ourselves. When we are filled with self, there is simply no way for us to experience contact with our Higher Power.

The "emptying" of our pitcher, of course, is the practice of inventorying our defects, sharing them with another, praying for their removal, and surrendering to the fact that the love of God is the only power that can truly change our lives. We are so fortunate, also, to be with others on this spiritual journey. Left to our own devices, many of us would return to the spell of our old ideas almost without realizing it. Our readings, our friends, and the discipline we have developed support our efforts to make a daily advancement along the journey.

Today, breathe in deeply an awareness of the Great Spirit and exhale the selfish desires that prevent your "pitcher" from being filled with the joy within. Rest assured that the supply to meet your spiritual desires is unlimited. Make room within yourself, and it will appear.

Weekly Journal: Ego

Initial Thoughts:

_____
_____
_____
_____
_____

Daily Reflections:

_____
_____
_____
_____
_____
_____
_____
_____
_____
_____
_____
_____
_____

Week's Conclusions:

_____
_____
_____
_____
_____

Dear Friend,

It has been said that laughter can illuminate the darkness of a closed mind. I have always loved and admired comedians, mainly for their ability to get me to laugh at myself. It's always such a relief and gives me such a sense of freedom. I now understand that I am laughing at the seriousness of my own ego.

I am certain that God has a wonderful sense of humor. Why else would the ego exist in the first place? My theory is that God wants a continuous series of vaudeville acts and comedy routines. God simply picks one of us up, winds up the ego, places us back on the stage of life, and the show begins . . .

"Hello, my name is _____, and I'm important! Look at my resume! Look at my body! Look at my car! Look at my bank account! Hi, all of you. I bet you would give anything to get to know me. Well, I already have enough friends! Ha! Ha! Ha! My problems are unique. I am engaged in a truly epic struggle. I am the center of the universe, and the universe refuses to acknowledge me. I could write the greatest novel ever written or save the planet, but I am presently thinking of suicide!"

With great love, God allows laughter to place a mirror in front of us, letting us see our egos as the frauds they are. We can take our last bow and exit stage right. Waiting in the wings, arms extended to embrace us, is our Higher Power. As we surrender to the comfort of Divine Love, we intuitively know that the real show is about to begin.

Weekly Journal: Change

Initial Thoughts:

_____
_____
_____
_____
_____

Daily Reflections:

_____
_____
_____
_____
_____
_____
_____
_____
_____
_____
_____
_____

Week's Conclusions:

_____
_____
_____
_____
_____

Dear Friend,

Have you ever resisted change? Did you feel like telling the world to stop for a while and just leave things the way they were? Do you ever yearn for the good old days when everything seemed much simpler and less confusing? Do you like a routine where each day is similar to the one that just passed? All of us have experienced these thoughts and feelings at one time or another. But to progress spiritually, we must learn to see change as it really is: God's reality.

When we think about the universe, it is obvious that one constant element since the beginning of time has been change. The entire system continuously expands. Each day moves us along through another season. The cells in our bodies are in a constant state of change. Like it or not, change is the order of the day.

What we must control is our attitude toward change. When we flow with the changing spiritual reality of life, we are given the power to see God's plan in action. When our egos attempt to resist the change in order to exert some control over our lives, we suffer the pain and anxiety of having things not go our way.

A daily routine of letting go and letting God is the surest means of accepting, and even welcoming, change in our lives. Time spent drawing closer to our Higher Power allows us to harness our egos. Since our egos are what offer resistance to God's ever-changing reality, we are thus free to travel through our day with gratitude instead of resentment.

Weekly Journal: Inner Spirit

Initial Thoughts:

_____

_____

_____

_____

_____

Daily Reflections:

_____

_____

_____

_____

_____

_____

_____

_____

_____

_____

_____

_____

Week's Conclusions:

_____

_____

_____

_____

_____

Dear Friend,

Today, let's enjoy a beautiful Chinese proverb: "If there is light in the soul, there will be beauty in the person. If there is beauty in the person, there will be harmony in the house. If there is harmony in the house, there will be order in the nation. If there is order in the nation, there will be peace in the world."

As this proverb shows, everything begins with you and me. Our world begins with the center of our being and moves outward. When our soul is illumined, the way before us is smooth. We really do have the power to shape the world in which we exist. Instead of demanding that the world supply us with peace and happiness, we must turn within to search for our center of light. Once found, it can transform our world before our very eyes.

You were born to be a beacon penetrating the darkness of ignorance and separateness. Within you is the power to transform your life and the lives of others. We must learn to ignore the cynical and distrustful voice of our ego and take continuous steps along our spiritual path. Each day, we will set aside time for prayer and meditation. Surely, these are the guarantors of our spiritual progress.

Are you wondering if you really make a difference? Let me assure you that in your life, you make all the difference there is. Everything depends on you and your decision to find your Inner Light. Today, let's commit ourselves to a life of seeking. We will know the light!

Weekly Journal: Miracles

Initial Thoughts:

_____

_____

_____

_____

_____

Daily Reflections:

_____

_____

_____

_____

_____

_____

_____

_____

_____

_____

_____

Week's Conclusions:

_____

_____

_____

_____

_____

Dear Friend,

Sometimes we hear the word *miracle* used in such casual ways that we fail to see the magnificent reality of miracles in our lives. People have described a *miracle* as "a coincidence where God chooses to remain anonymous." Most likely, all of us can recall a number of such "coincidences." But instead of simply acknowledging these events in our lives as spiritual coincidences, why not use each opportunity to deepen our awareness of the presence of our Higher Power?

For example, after praying for help in a troubled relationship, you see it remarkably turn harmonious. Be sure to take the time to see the hand of God touching your life. Use the occasion to expand your faith in the unseen. If we really get honest with ourselves and practice looking for God in the daily happenings of our lives, we will begin to see all of life as a miracle. Instead of thinking of God as making an occasional appearance in our lives, we can develop an awareness of the all-ness of our Higher Power.

For, indeed, everything is of God. Each coincidence or miracle is available to us as a reminder that we are players on God's stage. All of life is the creation of our Higher Power. We need to develop our spiritual vision so that we can look beyond the material world of our egos and become aware of a new level of existence.

At first, we may experience only occasional glimpses provided by coincidences. But these are just small steps toward the full awareness of the Divine Essence within us. Believe and you will see.

Weekly Journal: Honesty

Initial Thoughts:

_____
_____
_____
_____
_____

Daily Reflections:

_____
_____
_____
_____
_____
_____
_____
_____
_____
_____
_____
_____

Week's Conclusions:

_____
_____
_____
_____
_____

Dear Friend,

Today, let's pause for a while and think about the importance of honesty in reaching our spiritual goals.

At the first level, we see how not telling the truth during the course of our day causes great disharmony and distrust among those around us. We also come to understand the remorse and loss of self-esteem that results from such behavior.

At the next level, we acknowledge the absolute necessity for honesty in establishing any contact whatsoever with our Higher Power. In short, we open our eyes to the tremendous value of honesty in *all* areas of our lives. At this stage, our honesty is focused on the telling of the truth. In other words, we will speak only what we believe to be the truth.

As we open our minds further, however, we may discover that some of the ideas we have held are wrong. We are like those who lived before the discovery that the world is round. They honestly believed that the world was flat. They were not lying, but they also were not speaking the truth. As we examine our old ideas and acknowledge much of the fallibility in them, we begin to see honesty as the seeking of the truth.

Our spiritual lives will be measured over time by our ability and willingness to continuously scrutinize our ideas and motives. With rigorous honesty, we can bring to light half-truths and rationalizations that stand between us and our goals. The path of honesty leads to God.

Weekly Journal: Today

Initial Thoughts:

_____

_____

_____

_____

_____

Daily Reflections:

_____

_____

_____

_____

_____

_____

_____

_____

_____

_____

_____

Week's Conclusions:

_____

_____

_____

_____

_____

Dear Friend,

Today I have some questions for you. To make it easy, I'll start by telling you that the answer to all of them is the same. When would be a good day to try some meditation? When would be a good day to make amends for something that has been bothering you for a while? When would be a good day to call someone close and share some love? When would be a good day to talk to God at every opportunity? When would be a good day to end the day by reviewing how you might have behaved in a kinder and more loving manner?

Yes, the answer to all of the above is "Today." In fact, today is always the answer. All of your life exists right now! All of the power of the universe exists right now! To live in the now, to be totally consumed by the moment, is our ticket to freedom. How often in the course of a day do we have a sudden thought or inspiration such as, "I should really sign up for that retreat," or, "I ought to call my sister and tell her I'm sorry." For a brief second, we savor the clarity and truth of the moment. Then our ego inserts itself, vetoes the inspiration, and we go on complaining of being stuck in a rut.

Dear Friend, take the time to find the voice within. Clear away the debris of the past. Silence the boiling resentment and the roaring guilt. Strip the ego of its arsenal of fear and pride. Surrender to the silence and peace of the now. Touch a rose and allow the reality that you are touching a rose to be everything there is. And in that moment, you will be as free as the rose.

Weekly Journal: Freedom

Initial Thoughts:

_____

_____

_____

_____

_____

Daily Reflections:

_____

_____

_____

_____

_____

_____

_____

_____

_____

_____

_____

_____

Week's Conclusions:

_____

_____

_____

_____

_____

Dear Friend,

Have you ever been a prisoner? Some among us have, and we know that it is not pleasant. Perhaps the greatest pain is the loss of freedom. Four walls and a strict schedule planned by others. The central focus is "doing time." Finally, the day arrives. The gates are opened, and we are free! But what goes wrong? The emotional rush of being free is short lived, and we soon find life unmanageable and painful. The illusion of freedom leaves a sour taste in our mouths. We turn to ourselves for answers, and none are to be found.

Aren't we all prisoners in some way? Is true freedom an illusion or a burden? Inside our heads, aren't we trapped by the four walls made up of our old ideas? Haven't we told ourselves to "do time" until we get another job or relationship or place to live, and then everything will be okay? Where in the world, one asks, is this thing called "freedom?"

Who would ever guess that freedom comes from total surrender to a loving Higher Power? Instead of mastering our will, we attempt to do those things that will result in freedom from our own will. "Thy will, not mine!" is more than a theory. Day by day, step by step, we wrestle with ourselves to surrender. If we slip and take control back, we recognize it as soon as possible and then return to our individual spiritual journeys.

Now and then, we get glimpses of serenity and peace of mind. We come to realize that our efforts are indeed paying dividends. Remember, you are worth the work!

Weekly Journal: Letting Go

Initial Thoughts:

_____

_____

_____

_____

_____

Daily Reflections:

_____

_____

_____

_____

_____

_____

_____

_____

_____

_____

_____

_____

Week's Conclusions:

_____

_____

_____

_____

_____

Dear Friend,

An old-timer I knew had a favorite saying, which was, "It ain't the things you don't know that can kill you. It's knowing things for sure that just ain't so!"

Most of us are literally filled with ideas that "just ain't so." Some of them are about ourselves. Some are about other people. Many of them are about God, or perhaps the lack of a God. Unless we change these ideas, our world will remain the same. The problem facing us, or course, is that to change, we will have to admit that we have been mistaken about some things. Maybe a lot of things.

Being wrong is not our specialty. Perhaps being *wronged* but certainly not being *wrong*. Our pride conspires with our fear, and we cling desperately to old ideas. We hold them without reason. We are like the man who lived deep in a cave and was convinced the whole world must be dark. He refused to go outside to see the sun that others talked about for fear that his theory about the world would be proven wrong.

Today, let us walk into the sun. Let us strip away old ideas as we might brush off stinging insects. The darkness of old, self-centered ideas has trapped us in a joyless world of danger and anxiety. With God as our friend, we can find the courage to shine the spotlight of truth on every part of ourselves.

We will hold back nothing. We will surrender to the truth of a new, God-centered world. We will trust in the assurances of others who have come before us, and we will know freedom at last.

Weekly Journal: Kindness

Initial Thoughts:

_____

_____

_____

_____

_____

Daily Reflections:

_____

_____

_____

_____

_____

_____

_____

_____

_____

_____

_____

_____

Week's Conclusions:

_____

_____

_____

_____

_____

Dear Friend,

What is the power of a kind word? At first glance, it may seem insignificant. We ask ourselves, "One kind word? How could that make any impact on the world?"

Let's look for a moment at a tiny pebble thrown into a calm pool. It breaks the surface and sinks directly to the bottom. Not much effect there, you might say. But, look at the surface! Immediately after the pebble hits the water, concentric circles move out in all directions. The ripples extend farther and farther until they become imperceptible.

The entire pool has been affected by the presence of that pebble. Now, let's follow the ripple effect of one kind word. Imagine yourself in the waiting room at the doctor's office. You offer a kind word to the person sitting next to you who is absorbed with worry about his doctor visit.

That bit of cheer is overheard by seven other patients and a nurse who happens to be nearby. Each of them is touched in a positive way, and later, without realizing it, they find themselves extending kind words or looks to others they encounter. And those people brighten up a bit and extend themselves to one or two others. One of them is a messenger delivering a package to the office where you work. He is particularly pleasant to your grumpy office manager.

You arrive back at the office after your appointment and are quite surprised when the office manager drops by your desk and asks with genuine concern how you are feeling. That single kind word has come back full circle. What is the power of a kind word in your life? Find out today!

Weekly Journal: Loss

Initial Thoughts:

_____

_____

_____

_____

_____

Daily Reflections:

_____

_____

_____

_____

_____

_____

_____

_____

_____

_____

_____

_____

Week's Conclusions:

_____

_____

_____

_____

_____

Dear Friend,

Have you suffered a loss recently? Perhaps you have experienced the passing of a loved one or are going through a serious health, professional or financial setback.

We know these painful experiences come to everyone. However, when they actually happen to us, we need to remember to maintain contact with our Higher Power and with the spiritual reserves within us. Otherwise, the loss is likely to overpower us and leave us in a state of despair and hopelessness. Even though the immediate days and weeks ahead are going to be painful, we have the resources to go through them with dignity and grace.

Let's not ask that the pain be removed. Instead, let's seek the strength and courage to walk through the pain in a hopeful and loving manner. We can nurture ourselves within the fundamental truth that all is well in God's plan. We are being called upon to discover the greater strengths within us. We are being prepared to render future assistance to others with similar problems. We are being asked to exercise trust, patience and hope in quantities that we never dreamed we had. These are the times that measure our progress and that confirm our faith in God.

Today, seek solace in God and in the realization of your true nature. We must learn to release our attachments to people and events. Our loved ones and our futures are in the hands of God. The Divine Comforter loves you and makes available the spiritual resources to carry you in these difficult times.

Weekly Journal: Healing Spirit

Initial Thoughts:

_____
_____
_____
_____
_____

Daily Reflections:

_____
_____
_____
_____
_____
_____
_____
_____
_____
_____
_____
_____

Week's Conclusions:

_____
_____
_____
_____
_____

Dear Friend,

I read recently that medical doctors have demonstrated that a focus on the spiritual condition of their patients causes significant improvement in recovery rates. Prior to surgery, for example, doctors arrange for trained staff to spend time reading and praying with patients. These patients are more comfortable, relaxed and optimistic than others. The results are fewer complications and speedier recoveries.

There is great healing power in the spiritual life. The body itself is in a constant state of renewal, repair and healing. In most cases, the processes are automatic. That is, until you and I use our minds to disrupt the natural flow of events. When we subject our bodies to the stress of worry, anger, resentment, and fear, we greatly reduce the healing power within us. When we resent or fear a current physical ailment, we direct negative energy to the troubled area and add to the burden significantly.

Let's try to accept illness or injury with grace and dignity. Remember that we are in the hands of God, the Great Healer. Through prayer and meditation, we can open the natural channels of the body to allow the healing energy to flow within us. We train our minds to think about health, not sickness. We are in concert with our doctors. We picture health returning to us. We relax and turn our attention to others. We ask for God's grace for ourselves and for those about us. We know the power of God, and we are at peace.

Weekly Journal: Balance

Initial Thoughts:

_____

_____

_____

_____

_____

Daily Reflections:

_____

_____

_____

_____

_____

_____

_____

_____

_____

_____

_____

Week's Conclusions:

_____

_____

_____

_____

_____

Dear Friend,

I am sure that you have a very busy day ahead of you. So much to do and so little time! Yet, you have taken a few moments to read these words. Perhaps you are beginning to realize that time spent on your spiritual self will bring efficiency to all your daily tasks. It works; it really does.

In spite of your schedule today, take the time for quiet. Begin to know that a God-calmness is within your reach. Thank God for your life and all its blessings. Ask for blessings for everyone you meet today. Be aware that the center of your being is filled with the Divine Spirit and the calmness within this space is forever.

As you move through your day, rely on the stability of your spiritual center. When events start to tip the balance, return your thoughts to God. Pray only for calmness and the grace to treat others with dignity. Pursue your tasks with the assuredness of a Divine Representative. Claim the peace that is yours. Remind yourself that you are a child of God and that God's grace is always available to help you through the ups and downs of the day. Accept your role as that of God's agent. Simply do your best and leave the results in the hands of your Higher Power.

Tonight, return to the quiet within. Ask for the vision to see your day from a spiritual perspective. Look for the instances where you were kind or helpful. Acknowledge God's presence in the difficult situations that were handled with quiet confidence. Begin to recognize his greatness within you. It's there.

Weekly Journal: Ego

Initial Thoughts:

_____

_____

_____

_____

_____

Daily Reflections:

_____

_____

_____

_____

_____

_____

_____

_____

_____

_____

_____

Week's Conclusions:

_____

_____

_____

_____

_____

Dear Friend,

Did you ever think of yourself as having either plenty of energy or not enough? In a sense, we are all packages of energy that we call "Life." From a spiritual perspective, our true energy source is the spark of Divinity that burns within us. When we are centered on this source, we move effortlessly through a day. Events don't tire us as they do on other days. At the end of the day, we are still centered and are grateful for the efficiency and ease created by letting go and letting God.

But what happens on all those other days? Most likely, our old friend, our ego, takes over and leads us through a self-centered day. Cut off from our Divine Source, our character defects act as energy leaks and begin to drain us. Each angry thought or action robs some of our energy and simply throws it away. Each lustful thought or action takes more of this energy and wastes it. Every greedy or envious emotion taps our limited supply of energy and leaves us closer to empty. As we move through our day, the world and its people drain us, and in true ego-driven fashion, we blame them!

When the world controls us, it does so by taking our energies. Our life force itself is scattered into the atmosphere instead of providing us with its vital and spiritual nourishment. We are angry, and we are tired. Life is too much for us. Let us always return to the God within and allow the healing energy to bathe us in Divine Love. This is our life force, and it is ours alone. Remember to cherish and keep it!

Weekly Journal: Creativity

Initial Thoughts:

_____
_____
_____
_____
_____

Daily Reflections:

_____
_____
_____
_____
_____
_____
_____
_____
_____
_____
_____
_____

Week's Conclusions:

_____
_____
_____
_____
_____

Dear Friend,

Do you have any idea how truly creative you are? Often, the cares and burdens of life can stifle or block one's creative essence. When this happens, it is easy to think of ourselves as rather mundane and unimaginative beings. You are much more than a plodding shell making it to work each day and returning home to bed. Without realizing it, we may have buried our creativity under a self-imposed survival struggle.

It is a great tragedy when something like this happens, for we were created to create. Inside of you is a unique package of creativity. It was placed there by God. From it will come your own special, wonderful contribution to the world. You were placed here to add to the world, not to merely survive by taking from it. Your creativity can be released by placing all your trust in your Higher Power.

Dear Friend, the total you is limitless. As you take the steps to draw closer to the Divine Spirit, the shackles binding you to mere survival in the material world will be unlocked. A path will then be opened through which your creative energy can, at last, flow. Inspiration will occur regularly. Problem solving will become fun. You will eagerly look forward to each day. Thus inspired, you will draw even closer to the Universal Spirit. The magnitude of your creative energy expands. Your life becomes truly joyful. You realize fully that God is doing for you that which you only dreamed of before.

In these times, you come to see that the joy of living is indeed the joy of creating. Dear Friend, you are the guardian of a magnificent gift to all of us. Please unwrap it and share it. We love you!

Weekly Journal: Anger

Initial Thoughts:

_____
_____
_____
_____
_____

Daily Reflections:

_____
_____
_____
_____
_____
_____
_____
_____
_____
_____
_____
_____

Week's Conclusions:

_____
_____
_____
_____
_____

Dear Friend,

One of the most difficult human emotions is anger. Anger can cause us great pain and has the power to damage human relationships like no other emotion. Yet, what are we to do?

Things happen in the world that anger us. Are we to accept everything, even if we feel some things are wrong, just to avoid anger? Of course not. Perhaps the answer lies in looking at the difference between *anger* and *being angry*.

The anger within us probably has come from many sources. There may be social injustices that have upset us. We may have been frightened, embarrassed, or treated badly in the past. The anger within is a tremendous force. We can release some of it, but most of us will always have a store of anger lying within.

The spiritual answer to what to do with this reservoir of anger is to transform its energy into loving and constructive actions. We can pray for God to save us from being angry. We can have anger, but we do not become angry people. Through prayer and the resulting discipline, we can become energized to redress situations or right certain wrongs, but in a peaceful and God-centered manner.

Today, let's pray to understand our anger. Ask God for the power to refrain from angry acts or words. We seek the patience to curtail action until we establish contact with our Higher Power. Thus, centered in the peace and understanding of the Divine Spirit, we can pray for guidance in how best to proceed. When so inspired, we can use the spiritual energy to act in a loving and straightforward manner.

Weekly Journal: Inner Peace

Initial Thoughts:

_____
_____
_____
_____
_____

Daily Reflections:

_____
_____
_____
_____
_____
_____
_____
_____
_____
_____
_____
_____

Week's Conclusions:

_____
_____
_____
_____
_____

Dear Friend,

Let's focus for a moment on the word *quiet*. When you were small, your parents no doubt were often telling you to "be quiet." It's that way with most kids. Children are enthusiastic and noisy, and grown-ups are constantly trying to maintain some kind of order and peace.

If you were like my friends and I, the warning's effect wouldn't last long. Only minutes after being told to "be quiet," we would be just as loud as before. Eventually, an angry adult would confront us face-to-face, and we would quiet down for a while longer. Most of the time, though, it was simply impossible to be quiet for any extended period of time. It was as if we were powerless over being quiet.

Now that we're adults ourselves, we are able to refrain from loud laughing and talking, but what about "loud thinking?" Have we managed to gain the same control over annoying and upsetting thoughts? Most of us would have to admit that we have a way to go when it comes to inner quiet.

Today, let's go through our regular workday or whatever, but let's also maintain a new level of quiet within. We can do this simply by deciding to do it! We really can! After a time of prayer in the morning, let's begin to breathe deeply into the troubled thinking whenever it appears. Every time it returns, simply breathe into it and ask God for quiet within.

Throughout the day, let's continue to concentrate on breathing deeply into disturbing thoughts and praying for quiet within. Begin to see how intensely practical spiritual balance really is. The energy we have wasted in the past in worrying over tormenting thoughts can now be spent in useful tasks. We are in God's hands, and all is well!

Weekly Journal: Belief

Initial Thoughts:

_____

_____

_____

_____

_____

Daily Reflections:

_____

_____

_____

_____

_____

_____

_____

_____

_____

_____

_____

_____

Week's Conclusions:

_____

_____

_____

_____

_____

Dear Friend,

Do you ever struggle with believing in God? Do you find yourself doubting that a loving Higher Power is really available for you? Do you look around and conclude that there is simply no evidence for any belief at all? If so, perhaps it is your "Logical" mind that has taken over. Sometimes, without realizing it, we become scientific about our spirituality. Since few of us will ever experience a sudden and powerful spiritual experience, we will have to overcome the doubting "Logical" mind in other ways.

First, we must remember the results we had in our lives when we tried living without a belief in a Higher Power. For most of us, this experience was lonely, painful and totally unrewarding. We were frustrated continually by unmet needs and unfair people. Life lacked any meaning or purpose. Generally, circumstances brought us to our knees, and we were confronted with an inescapable conclusion. We were going to have to change our minds about the existence of God or face dreadful consequences.

Driven by circumstances rather than by logic, we decided to believe in something beyond ourselves. The results in our lives were miraculous. The evidence of the existence of God appears to us through the process of believing. We must always go beyond our ego-driven minds and surrender to the simple premise that our understanding of God will come from experiencing this Power in our lives. Let us each day decide to believe.

Weekly Journal: Temptations

Initial Thoughts:

_____

_____

_____

_____

_____

Daily Reflections:

_____

_____

_____

_____

_____

_____

_____

_____

_____

_____

_____

Week's Conclusions:

_____

_____

_____

_____

_____

Dear Friend,

Did you ever think to yourself, if only Adam hadn't eaten that apple? Then our lives would be free of all these struggles and problems. We would be sitting pretty in the Garden of Eden, sharing a pizza. Or am I the only one who worries about these important things?

Rather than resenting Adam (or Eve, for tempting him), perhaps we should look at how well we handle temptation ourselves. If we were completely honest, we would have to admit that we wouldn't last long in the Garden either. Why is it that temptation plagues us daily?

No doubt each of us has one or more constant temptations. Whether they stem from greed, lust, anxiety or pride, we know what they are and what they have done to our lives. Just when we think we are free, there arises an urge, an overpowering thought, a desire or craving, a sudden impulse to engage in something that we know we will regret later.

Generally speaking, the simple hard truth is that temptation exists because there is something that we are not yet willing to give up. We may be almost willing, or ready to be willing, but we're not there yet! In this condition, we are blocked from God's help. We cannot be in two places at once. We cannot serve our own desires and also experience God's will. We must choose, and we must be willing to go through the pain of not getting our way. The pain is temporary, and the joy is forever.

You are much stronger than you realize. Today, let us unconditionally seek God's help in meeting whatever temptations are put in our paths.

Weekly Journal: Intuition

Initial Thoughts:

_____

_____

_____

_____

_____

Daily Reflections:

_____

_____

_____

_____

_____

_____

_____

_____

_____

_____

_____

Week's Conclusions:

_____

_____

_____

_____

Dear Friend,

In the workplace, we might encounter something called a "brain-storming session." In it, a group gets together and tries to solve a problem by advancing one idea after another. The theory is that one idea will trigger another and then another. Eventually, someone will come up with a good solution. The results are generally mixed. Nevertheless, "brainstorming" is popular because it gives everyone a chance to participate. Sometimes all the voices are going at once, and it's hard to remember the original problem.

In our personal lives, our brains seem to love the concept of "brainstorming." In my head, it sometimes sounds like a committee of twelve up there. Life continues to throw problems our way, however, and they require solutions. Our normal approach is to attack a problem just by thinking about it! Sometimes we get a solution; most times we just worry and spin our wheels. Throughout it all, we are in a state of extreme agitation.

Within us, there is another method of addressing problems. We find it on the spiritual path. It is called *intuition*. To get to the intuitive level within us, we must first stop struggling with any and all problems. We humbly acknowledge that a greater wisdom lies within us. Instead of demanding solutions, we seek the closeness of our Higher Power. In the great silence of conscious contact, we will find either answers or patience. Either way, we are content!

Weekly Journal: Humility

Initial Thoughts:

_____
_____
_____
_____
_____

Daily Reflections:

_____
_____
_____
_____
_____
_____
_____
_____
_____
_____
_____
_____

Week's Conclusions:

_____
_____
_____
_____
_____

Dear Friend,

For most of us, the process of acquiring a measure of humility is quite painful. Often, it is only through a series of humiliating events that we begin to have even a glimpse of it. If this is so, then humiliating events must be important to our progress on the spiritual path. But, how can we ever come to welcome humiliation as a positive force? Perhaps we need to look at the difference between "humility" and "Humiliation."

In order to understand and fully accept, for example, that God is everything and we are nothing, we must exercise humility. Humility tames our ego and enables us to see spiritual truths and to rejoice in them. When spiritual truths conflict with our egotistical ideas about the world and ourselves, then we must be brought down to size through humiliation. Either way, we end up confronting the truth. One way is serene, the other, painful. The choice is ours.

Today, let's pray for a total absence of pride and our insistence on being right. Let's accept the world as God created it and seek to bring harmony wherever we walk. Let's smile and be grateful for the painful humiliations that have opened our eyes to the magnificent reality of our Higher Power. We truly are Children of God engaged in a mighty endeavor to seek the truth about ourselves and our origins. Humility can shine a bright light through the darkness ahead.

Weekly Journal: God Centered

Initial Thoughts:

_____

_____

_____

_____

_____

Daily Reflections:

_____

_____

_____

_____

_____

_____

_____

_____

_____

_____

_____

_____

Week's Conclusions:

_____

_____

_____

_____

Dear Friend,

Have you ever felt that your life has no meaning and that it is going nowhere? Does it seem that there is no purpose in the universe and that the world is just a bunch of selfish people taking advantage of each other? Are you the only one without a set of instructions for the game of life? Are you lost and afraid to admit it? Do you feel it is you against the world and that you are being overpowered?

Perhaps we can best understand why things look so out of sorts by examining just one single part of your life. Please honestly answer this question: "Today, what lies at the center of your life?" Do you see yourself at the center with the world and its people and its events all around you? If so, doesn't it seem that everything is happening to you?

When we try to view the world with us as the center, Dear Friend, it will always look distorted and frightening. This is because we are making a mistake. In the 1500s, astronomers began to see the sun as the center of our solar system. Before that time, they had placed the Earth at the center. Since the sun really is the center of our system, everything suddenly began making sense. Earth's path and those of the other planets were quite orderly and could be understood.

The true center of our existence is God. We are part of God's divine plan, and everything is as it should be. We co-exist with God and derive our energy from this infinite source. Make God your center, and you will have a true view of your world.

Weekly Journal: Surrender

Initial Thoughts:

_____

_____

_____

_____

_____

Daily Reflections:

_____

_____

_____

_____

_____

_____

_____

_____

_____

_____

_____

Week's Conclusions:

_____

_____

_____

_____

_____

Dear Friend,

I have a wonderful poster of several brightly colored hot-air balloons carrying people aloft and across the Arizona desert. The sky is so blue, and there are majestic mountains in the distance.

It is exciting to watch the launching of these beautiful airborne chariots. After much preparation, the balloon begins to fill with the heated air and soon is straining against the tie-down ropes. The lucky passengers climb into the gondola and stand looking out from their special perch. The ropes are untied, but one remains tangled. The balloon strains to take off but cannot until the last rope is freed. After a few moments, the troublesome knot is loosened, and the balloon rises effortlessly skyward. There it is free to move with the winds of God.

Within us also is a force eager to be free from the restraints of the material world. We were born with the innate desire to soar once again to the heights of closeness with our Divine Spirit. The power to rise already lies within us, but we must make the necessary preparations.

We must surrender to the fact that we, on our own, cannot rise even one centimeter above the reality of the material world. Neither our money nor our personal power can help us. To rise, we must cut all the ties that bind us to the visible world. The lines tying us to greed, envy, alcohol, lust, drugs, pride, anger or whatever must all be totally loosened. Just one remaining line can keep us on the ground and permanently frustrate the longing of our souls. Let go of everything and rise toward perfect unity. You are loved.

Weekly Journal: Ego/Death

Initial Thoughts:

_____

_____

_____

_____

_____

Daily Reflections:

_____

_____

_____

_____

_____

_____

_____

_____

_____

_____

_____

_____

_____

Week's Conclusions:

_____

_____

_____

_____

_____

Dear Friend,

"It is by dying that one awakens to eternal life." So says the last line of the Prayer of St. Francis. Generally, a discussion of dying makes us uncomfortable. But why should it? After all, we use the words "die" and "death" all the time: "I'm dying to see that movie!" "I almost died when he asked me to the dance!" "I was so mortified, I could have died!"

Clearly, St. Francis was referring to the death of our egos rather than of our human bodies. It is the ego and the ego alone that keeps us away from God. The ego tells us that we can exist as separate beings and that we each have a unique identity and perspective on the world. When we are able – through reflection, prayer, and meditation – to set ourselves free from our egotistical ideas, we are actually killing our egos.

At first, we are very apprehensive about what will happen to us if the ego dies. We might feel that we will have no existence at all without it. When we walk through the fear and do the work, however, we find the miracle of true life lying directly on the other side of the ego. We then celebrate our freedom from many of our old ideas.

Death is necessary in order to give life its meaning. And fear of death may only be the fear of never having lived. Once we glimpse the other side of ego life, we begin to see the eternal nature of God and, therefore, all life.

Weekly Journal: Fear

Initial Thoughts:

_____

_____

_____

_____

_____

Daily Reflections:

_____

_____

_____

_____

_____

_____

_____

_____

_____

_____

_____

Week's Conclusions:

_____

_____

_____

_____

_____

Dear Friend,

Today is the window through which we can learn to see everything about our existence. Today is the package of time in which we always exist. Our minds cause us great trouble by taking us out of today. Our fearful thinking tells us to worry about tomorrow, and our guilty thinking tells us to anguish about yesterday. When our energies are split in this way, we cannot focus ourselves in the moment. But the moment is all there is or ever will be.

Let's begin the practice of disciplining our minds today. After all, why should your mind decide what you think about? We don't let our legs take us anywhere they want to go, do we? Well, our minds belong to us just like our legs. Possibly we have never realized that we can actually take control of what our minds think about.

Since most of us have spent a good part of our lives almost at the mercy of our own minds, we will clearly face a challenge when we try to corral these wayward travelers. But nothing will pay greater dividends, for by doing so, we are at last addressing the true cause of our discomfort in this world and beginning the contact with our eternal spiritual natures.

To take control, we must acquire the discipline of silencing the mind. This is what prayer and meditation are all about. Through daily practice, we slowly gain the ability to remove ourselves from the clutches of uncontrolled thinking. By painstakingly untying each bond to our mind, we slowly enter the realm of "God-centeredness."

Weekly Journal: Keep It Simple

Initial Thoughts:

_____
_____
_____
_____
_____

Daily Reflections:

_____
_____
_____
_____
_____
_____
_____
_____
_____
_____
_____

Week's Conclusions:

_____
_____
_____
_____
_____

Dear Friend,

You've probably heard the advice, "Keep it simple!" This adage offers us profound insight into how to succeed on the spiritual path.

In a way, simplicity is the exact opposite of itself – it is anything but simple. In fact, it is quite difficult. Think of a great baseball hitter or a graceful dancer. They make their performances look so easy and simple. What we don't see are the hours, months and years of practice that produce that simplicity of motion.

On the spiritual path, simplicity is the result of our striving and praying. I read once about a spiritual master who suggested to a novice this spiritual goal. "When you wash a glass," he said, "just wash the glass." His advice sounds so simple. Yet, following it is so very, very difficult.

Isn't it true that when you and I wash a glass, we are washing with our hands, but we are thinking about what has to be done later or what we forgot to do earlier? In a spiritual sense, we are not present at the washing of the glass. The lesson of simplicity is to always be present in the Now and to focus 100% on the task at hand.

This type of "simple" life contains the key to freedom from the problems of the past and the future. The problems themselves are not solved in the traditional sense, they are simply removed because they are not part of "washing the glass."

There is no reason that glass washing can't be enjoyable. Joy comes from the inner awareness that we are close to our Higher Power and that we are lucky to be alive and to be performing any task at all.

Weekly Journal: Compassion

Initial Thoughts:

_____

_____

_____

_____

_____

Daily Reflections:

_____

_____

_____

_____

_____

_____

_____

_____

_____

_____

_____

Week's Conclusions:

_____

_____

_____

_____

_____

Dear Friend,

I once overheard a man make a most disquieting comment about his life. "The world," he lamented, "is so cold and cruel. I have decided to harden my heart." This is a terrible punishment to impose on oneself. A hardened heart is surely a guarantee of a sad and lonely life. As we think, so shall it be!

If we can only learn to allow our hearts a greater role in our lives, we shall certainly enter a world of great caring and compassion. Our self-centered ego would have us look out for and protect only the center of all its attention – itself. Others are merely tools for achieving its ends or obstacles that block it. To the ego, compassion is a curse word.

But surely compassion is part of our original state. By nature, each of us is a very compassionate person. As we have gone through the material world, we have learned to suppress our compassion in favor or reaching selfish ends, even at the expense of others. But if we succeed by this method, does it guarantee happiness? No, our happiness is short-lived and illusory because part of us cares about other people. Part of us can't forget what we have done. Part of us now wants a voice. Our ego is frantic and is looking for a way to gag that part.

Let's draw close to our Higher Power and pray for guidance. Let's allow God to set us free from our self-centered ends and give us faith and trust in the truth of the universe. Only then can we truly become instruments of God's peace.

Let our hearts rejoice as we release the store of compassion within us that has been so patiently waiting for the chance to change our world.

Weekly Journal: Honesty

Initial Thoughts:

_____

_____

_____

_____

_____

Daily Reflections:

_____

_____

_____

_____

_____

_____

_____

_____

_____

_____

_____

Week's Conclusions:

_____

_____

_____

_____

_____

Dear Friend,

We all have heard the beautiful words, "And the truth shall set you free!" Did you ever wonder what exactly this freedom is? From what are we being set free? Is it freedom from sadness? Freedom from hunger? Freedom from fear? Freedom from loneliness? Most likely, it is freedom from our old ideas, from our illusions about the world and ourselves. True freedom is the end of the deception that we exist as separate beings from God. A key element in obtaining this freedom is honesty.

In a sense, honesty is the willingness to always seek the truth within ourselves. When you fearlessly pursue an honest evaluation of yourself, you will be set free from old ideas that have plagued you for years, if not decades. Today, you may be the prisoner of perceptions that bombard you with emotion-jarring pronouncements such as, "The world is unfair to me! I am no good! Certain people and situations intimidate me! I can't do it! Everyone else is cheating at life, why shouldn't I? God loves everyone but me!"

Dear Friend, unlike material growth, spiritual growth consists of shedding instead of acquiring. We are seeking nothing in our spiritual quest because we already have everything we need. We simply don't believe it. The reason we don't believe it is because of the false ideas we have collected in the course of our lives. Through honesty, we can begin the difficult process of shedding our ego-centered ideas about ourselves and the world. As we do so, our true nature can begin to reveal itself.

Inside of you is a brilliant light of love, full of creative energy and intuition. This Divine energy source awaits the chance to serve you. Your task is to honestly identify and then discard the untruths that block its path. God loves you!

Weekly Journal: Present/Freedom

Initial Thoughts:

_____

_____

_____

_____

_____

Daily Reflections:

_____

_____

_____

_____

_____

_____

_____

_____

_____

_____

_____

_____

Week's Conclusions:

_____

_____

_____

_____

_____

Dear Friend,

Many of us are in a seemingly never-ending struggle with our past. We drag the heavy baggage of past events around with us, telling ourselves that we will never be free of our past until we "deal" with it. As a result, the past greatly controls our present. We try to make amends to those we have wronged or to forgive those who have hurt us. But still we are stuck in the past. How can we move forward?

Imagine yourself on a giant roller coaster. The car has just climbed to the highest point in the ride, gone over the top, and is pointing almost straight down. You are hanging on for dear life as it hurtles down the track, picking up speed, faster and faster and faster! Now, tell me: At this moment, are you wondering how your life might have been better if only your mother had loved you more? Or, if your father hadn't left home when you were little? Or, if you had been born with a different body or mind? I doubt it. Most likely, you are totally consumed with the moment, experiencing fear, excitement and exhilaration all at one.

Clearly, it is possible to get out from under the spell of our past. This is an important thing to realize. In fact, we are probably much freer than we know. We are like the prisoner whose jail cell has been unlocked after many, many years of confinement. He has paid his dues, and there is nothing holding him except his decision to walk through the door. We must claim our freedom, or it simply will not be real for us. Hand in hand with God, we must step through that doorway to confront the demands of our past and refuse to submit.

Weekly Journal: Letting God

Initial Thoughts:

_____

_____

_____

_____

_____

Daily Reflections:

_____

_____

_____

_____

_____

_____

_____

_____

_____

_____

_____

Week's Conclusions:

_____

_____

_____

_____

_____

Dear Friend,

And elderly woman was coming out of a supermarket, struggling to carry a heavy bag of groceries. Each step she took was slower and slower. Seeing the situation, a young man stopped and asked if he could carry the bag for her. She smiled and handed it to him and then easily accompanied him to her car. After he placed the bag in the trunk, she thanked him and got into her car. Wearing a very peaceful look on her face, she drove off. The young man walked into the market with a big smile on his face.

Perhaps life appears to have placed a very heavy burden on your shoulders. At times, it is just so hard to continue. All your energy seems to be used up just carrying the burden. You pray that somehow something will happen to change your lot. But it does not.

Let us pause and look at the burden itself. Doesn't it consist primarily of worry, fear, resentment, and doubt? Haven't we placed these extra loads on our own shoulders? Let us imagine our Higher Power standing by our sides, arms outstretched, patiently waiting for us to return these burdens to their rightful place.

We are never alone. You and I have within us a spiritual essence that is constantly connected to God. We must daily take the time to make ourselves aware of this connection. When we do so, we are free to move through life as God intended. God loves you.

Weekly Journal: Inventory

Initial Thoughts:

_____

_____

_____

_____

_____

Daily Reflections:

_____

_____

_____

_____

_____

_____

_____

_____

_____

_____

_____

Week's Conclusions:

_____

_____

_____

_____

_____

Dear Friend,

How often do you make a list of the things that are blocking you from God? Sometimes our lives can be compared to the gutters on a roof. When properly cleaned, those gutters easily catch water from the roof and send it down to the ground. But over time, leaves, twigs, and dirt begin to pile up in them. If ignored, the gutter becomes blocked. Water backs up and can damage the roof. There is nothing wrong with the gutter itself, it just needs to be cleaned.

Perhaps, my friend, there is nothing wrong with you either. You just need to do some maintenance on your relationship with God. Stop wasting time trying to blame someone for the blockage or trying to find the deeper meaning of the blockage. Simply accept your situation and take the practical steps to re-open a channel to God.

Review you anger, resentments and fears. If you live in anger, forgive. If you have harmed others, make amends. List all the things in your life for which you are grateful. Stop and clean the gutters of your spiritual home so that the rains of adversity cannot dampen your tranquility.

Weekly Journal: Faith

Initial Thoughts:

_____

_____

_____

_____

_____

Daily Reflections:

_____

_____

_____

_____

_____

_____

_____

_____

_____

_____

_____

_____

Week's Conclusions:

_____

_____

_____

_____

_____

Dear Friend,

The other day I was thinking about when I was a young Boy Scout and was first shown a compass. The Scout Leader was teaching us how to find our way in the woods. He explained that the needle would always point to the north and, because of that, we could easily navigate. How comforting it was to simply put the compass in my pocket and know that I now had the power to find my own way through even the darkest woods.

Unlike in my later years, I didn't raise my hand and ask the Scout Leader how the needle knew to point to the north. I didn't ask myself what would happen to me if I got a compass that pointed to the south. I didn't scare myself to death by thinking that the needle would stop working if a bear was nearby. I simply accepted the good news with a child's faith in the wisdom of adults.

Dear Friend, there exists a spiritual compass within each of us that was designed specifically to guide us through life. The great dilemma of human existence is how to be guided through life by that compass instead of willing our way through it with our minds. Rather than dwelling on intellectual theories that say that spiritual guidance cannot exist, we need to surrender to the fact that we are indeed lost in the vastness of life. From there, we can turn to God with a child-like faith.

Focus your energies on drawing close to God. Seek the stillness out of which the spiritual signal can be heard. Strive for the conscious awareness of God and then realize that you never have been lost because you are lovingly enfolded in the arms of the Divine Navigator.

Weekly Journal: Trust

Initial Thoughts:

_____

_____

_____

_____

_____

Daily Reflections:

_____

_____

_____

_____

_____

_____

_____

_____

_____

_____

_____

Week's Conclusions:

_____

_____

_____

_____

_____

Dear Friend,

Today is your day! On this day, the world has been laid out in all its splendor for you. Seek nothing, for everything already is yours. Take time in the morning to reward yourself with stillness. In the embracing quiet, know that your life is unfolding right on schedule and that you are cherished by a loving God.

Go about the business of your day as an instrument of your Higher Power. Seek guidance as you encounter those times set aside for your finances, your relationships, your profession, your health, and above all, your self-image. Relieve yourself of all concerns in these areas and give them to God – for that is where they belong, not on your shoulders. Your task is simply the doing, not the agonizing. The only way to accomplish this is by placing your trust in God, not in yourself.

A young man once asked me, "If I don't worry about myself, who will?" I know he was serious, but can you see the humor in that question? Worrying can only be done by our ego. Think of this, Dear Friend, as you draw close to the Divine Spirit. There is no such thing as spiritual worry. The ego illusion will be revealed in the presence of your true spiritual nature.

This is your day. Go forth with a God-centered awareness that many gifts await you. Be open to the sights and sounds of God's plan at work. Be of service to the world you can see, but take your joy from the hidden depths within. Know that you walk with a grateful dignity. You are a perfectly created creature, and your love can change the world.

Weekly Journal: Sharing

Initial Thoughts:

_____

_____

_____

_____

_____

Daily Reflections:

_____

_____

_____

_____

_____

_____

_____

_____

_____

_____

_____

Week's Conclusions:

_____

_____

_____

_____

_____

Dear Friend,

Do you have a secret about yourself that you have never shared with another person? You are not alone. Many of us have carried the burden of embarrassing or shameful incidents for years. Some of us have sworn to keep them a secret forever. This decision prevents us from ever developing a true relationship with another person. We always wonder what people will think of us once they know what we have done. Moreover, by not sharing with another, we have given our secrets extra power over us. We believe our secrets are so bad that they cannot be shared.

Even more damaging is what our secrets tell us about those close to us. The reason we have kept our secret is because no one can be trusted. We have, therefore, created a world of friends, relatives, and professional advisors who cannot be trusted. This is a very frightening world, indeed. And all of this is because our egos don't want our perfect reputation to be tarnished. Pride coupled with fear conspires to sentence us to permanent isolation.

A loving God provides the release from our problem. By placing our trust in our Higher Power, we are free to take the steps we never dared before. As we carefully choose and share with another, we are graced with the gift of self-forgiveness. We walk from the darkness of illusion into the sunshine of the truth.

Secrets constantly gnaw at the marrow of moral fiber and exact a terrible toll. Resolve today to begin your climb toward unity with God and your fellow travelers.

Weekly Journal: Money

Initial Thoughts:

_____

_____

_____

_____

_____

Daily Reflections:

_____

_____

_____

_____

_____

_____

_____

_____

_____

_____

_____

_____

Week's Conclusions:

_____

_____

_____

_____

Dear Friend,

Now what about money? Economists describe money as "access to goods and services." As money flows through our hands, each of us is fed, clothed, housed, transported, and amused. It could be viewed as the medium through which we interact with each other. One of us can build a house while another grows the food. Through the exchange of money, both can be housed and fed.

But what if we let money far exceed its intended purpose? What if we seek, if not worship, money as an end in itself? Can our fears, greed and selfishness make us need money so much that we trample on others? And can our dependence on money seriously get in the way of our dependence on God?

Money can be likened to water that flows into a lake. If it can't flow back out of the lake, it will become stagnant. In a similar way, a stagnant pool of money leads to showy displays of wealth and selfishness or turns us into misers who secretly hoard our money.

Let us redefine the word *money* in spiritual terms. Money is "access to service and good." Seek to increase your standard of *giving* over your standard of *living*. Even our own currency tells us, "In God We Trust."

Weekly Journal: Letting Go

Initial Thoughts:

_____

_____

_____

_____

_____

Daily Reflections:

_____

_____

_____

_____

_____

_____

_____

_____

_____

_____

_____

_____

Week's Conclusions:

_____

_____

_____

_____

_____

Dear Friend,

As we develop an awareness of the Spirit Within, we will notice that our world seems less painful and more open to us. This is because we are seeing the world from a new and different perspective: That of a God-centered person.

Such is the power of letting go. We can improve our view even further if we make a conscious decision to look for the God Spirit in others. Instead of judging others by their differences from us, we can start to see that everyone shares the same inner essence, the same Spirit Within.

When we look at others as fellow passengers on a spiritual journey, we are free to be one among many seeking inner peace. We can escape our old ideas of being less than or more than those around us. We come to realize that each of us is doing our best to handle the particular situation that life has given us.

Today, let's try and see our world as one large spiritual school where we are all doing our best to master the lesson that God has given us. Rest assured that the curriculum has been carefully planned, even though it rarely makes sense to us at the time. We must remember that the school was not designed to make us rich or important, but rather to bring us closer to our Higher Power.

Look to this day for your lessons. Seek to understand others as you do yourself. Be of assistance on the spiritual journey to those you might help. Experience the joy of living today.

Weekly Journal: Prayer

Initial Thoughts:

_____

_____

_____

_____

_____

Daily Reflections:

_____

_____

_____

_____

_____

_____

_____

_____

_____

_____

_____

_____

Week's Conclusions:

_____

_____

_____

_____

_____

Dear Friend,

Today, let's open our minds to a personal realization of the power of prayer in our lives. On one level, we may have many reasons for praying, such as asking for good health or help in getting a job. In the long run, however, we should be aware of the one nourishing constant that occurs every time we pray: Our minds are lifted up to God.

Without prayer, our thinking tends to stay focused on the ego center of our universe. When we go through our day in this condition, we inevitably find one thing after another that is not to our liking. We are always experiencing the pain and frustration of wanting things other than the way they are.

By establishing the daily practice of prayer, we literally "move" the mind from its perpetual preoccupation with self to the true center of our lives, our Higher Power. The practical results of this ritual are remarkable. The more time we spend in prayer, the more the world will seem in harmony with us. If we really try, we can accomplish every task in our day while simultaneously praying. After all, don't we now go through each day doing our assigned tasks and simultaneously keeping track of every unfair incident we encounter? Without missing a beat, we even plan revenge!

Developing the habit of prayer is like having an anchor in the stormy waters of life. As the ups and downs of each day attempt to exert their influence over our serenity and peace of mind, we can experience the stability provided by closeness to God.

Weekly Journal: Love

Initial Thoughts:

_____

_____

_____

_____

_____

Daily Reflections:

_____

_____

_____

_____

_____

_____

_____

_____

_____

_____

_____

_____

Week's Conclusions:

_____

_____

_____

_____

Dear Friend,

What is the power of the love within you and me? Isn't it far beyond anything we have yet experienced?

One of the beautiful results of spiritual growth is the widening of what was at first a channel into a full reservoir of love within each of us. Unfortunately, the world often teaches us to control this wonderful and natural love. We are taught that in order to "get ahead" and be "a success," we must selfishly look out for ourselves, even at the expense of others. We have each experienced the results of this philosophy: anxiety, hollow victories, a sense of disillusionment, envy, and a feeling of distrust for others.

As we go through life, many of us have concluded cynically that love is the last thing we need to help us deal with this confusing world. At some turning point in our lives, events force us to change our minds, and we discover that we were wrong. At that moment, we begin the process of spiritual freedom, which is freedom from our own ideas. As we discard old "truths," we move closer and closer to our true natures. We joyfully discover that love is the real guiding force within us. Let's take control away from that part of us that would seek to prevent this love from expressing itself.

Today, we can try to allow love to flow from us fearlessly. Let it flow unconditionally. Allow it to transform the world as we move through it. You are love.

Weekly Journal: Clarity

Initial Thoughts:

_____

_____

_____

_____

_____

Daily Reflections:

_____

_____

_____

_____

_____

_____

_____

_____

_____

_____

_____

_____

Week's Conclusions:

_____

_____

_____

_____

_____

Dear Friend,

Have you ever suffered the disappointment of opening a package of recently developed photos, only to find that most of them are out of focus? Sadly, you realize that you will never be able to re-capture those lost moments. Because each scene is blurred and vague, we almost always end up throwing away these pictures, and with them, the opportunity to preserve certain memorable events.

Fuzziness is not restricted to photos. The way we are living out our lives can also lack focus. When we are preoccupied with fear, anger, greed and envy, we go through our days with scattered actions and thoughts. We are lacking a quality that is essential to living a purposeful and focused life – *clarity*.

Clarity is a wonderful result of our spiritual efforts. Through meditation, prayer and letting go of old ways of thinking, we are able to clean house and get rid of the many distortions in our view of ourselves and the world. As we eliminate conflicting and distorted thinking, we are blessed with a clarity of purpose and energy that can transform our lives.

For the very first time, we are free to experience our true natures. Often, we are astounded at the simplicity and clarity of life itself. By living God's plan instead of trying to run the world ourselves, we can totally focus in the moment. The future and the past are no longer our concerns.

Weekly Journal: Letting Go

Initial Thoughts:

_____
_____
_____
_____
_____

Daily Reflections:

_____
_____
_____
_____
_____
_____
_____
_____
_____
_____
_____
_____

Week's Conclusions:

_____
_____
_____
_____
_____

Dear Friend,

"A rose, by any other name, would smell as sweet . . ." This wonderful line from Shakespeare's *Romeo and Juliet* speaks to a great truth about you and me.

No matter what we call ourselves, no matter what other people have called us, no matter what they may have written about us, we are forever children of God. A rose is a rose. And a child of God is a child of God. We can call the rose a tulip, but it will still smell as sweet as a rose. People may call you a loser, a failure, a bad child, a rotten person or many other painful names. You can choose to think these things of yourself, but it still doesn't alter the fact that you are a child of God.

Let's rejoice in this truth: It's never too late to begin anew. Today is the beginning of the rest of our lives. No matter what we have done yesterday, we can turn to our Higher Power today. We can discard any ideas about ourselves that tell us we are other than children of God. They have no stock with us because they are simply not true. Once we make a list of our old ideas and then discard them, we can enter the realm of our true natures.

In your travels today, try to go by a rose garden or a flower shop. Stop and look at the roses, beautiful creations of God. See in them the permanency of God's work. Know that nothing can take away a rose's fragrant smell.

Tonight, look deeply into your heart. Pierce the veil of illusion and give up those old ideas about yourself. God is in you.

Richard Beach

Richard "Sandy" Beach graduated from Yale University in 1953 and joined the U.S. Marine Corps at the tail end of the Korean War. He began a career as a jet fighter pilot - - a career that was ultimately shattered by 14 years of chronic alcoholism. In his struggle for sobriety, he experienced malnutrition, delirium tremens, and a six-month stay in a locked psychiatric ward.

In 1964, he was shown a spiritual path to recovery and has gained his insights and perspective from 50 years on the path of the Twelve Steps. For more than 45 years, he has been delivering spiritual lectures and workshops across America as well as in a number of foreign countries.

After completing a 20-year career as a lobbyist in Washington, D.C., he has retired to Tampa, Fl., where he has begun once again to put his spiritual thoughts on paper.

Of his life, Sandy says, "I know that I have never seen Heaven, but I have seen hell and made it back. And now this seems like Heaven."

FROM THE PUBLISHER

HOTCHKISS PUBLISHING

Hotchkiss Publishing is founded on the simple belief, so well expressed by Nelson Mandela in his 1994 inaugural speech, "as we let our own light shine, we unconsciously give other people permission to do the same." We hope that the words and ideas expressed by our authors remove fears, give hope, provide guidance and open doors thought to be closed. May they assist you during your journey through this life to discover the greatness within you.

Publishers Note:
Hotchkiss Publishing is pleased to be presenting some "Letters" which were written by Sandy Beach and offered here together for the first time. For many years Sandy has freely given of himself and shared his experience, strength, and hope without remuneration. It is in keeping with that tradition that these letters are being offered by the publisher with Sandy's blessing.

For information, please contact us at:
Hotchkiss Publishing
17 Frank Street
Branford, CT 06405
email: info@hotchkisspublishing.com
www.hotchkisspublishing.com

RICHARD "SANDY" JOHN BEACH

September 9, 1931 – September 28, 2014

Sandy was born in New Haven, CT on September 9, 1931. In his early teens, he contracted Polio and while in recovery he developed a fascination with magic. Sandy went on to be a high school track and field athlete with a passion for creative writing. In 1953, he graduated from Yale University with a degree in Spanish. He had six children, fifteen grandchildren, and two great-grandchildren. Four of his children survive him. For over a decade, Sandy flew as a fighter pilot with the U.S. Marines. His next career was as a speech writer and lobbyist for the Credit Union National Association in Washington, DC. He retired in Tampa, FL, where he enjoyed couples dancing and volunteered as a mentor for Big Brothers Big Sisters of America. On December 7, 1964 (Pearl Harbor Day) Sandy stopped drinking and began a deep and lasting belief in the spiritual power of Alcoholics Anonymous. Sandy became an inspired speaker in AA meetings large and small. He spoke about the principles of AA with a special blend of humor and wisdom all over the world. He created and taught an AA spiritual recovery workshop for men known as The Far Corners; true to it's name, men travelled near and far to learn from Sandy.